TRUCILLA'S
WEDDING

A RHYMOBIC

D1382502

The Writer and Illustrator who created this book:

CORINNE V. DAVIES, the middle child of three. Her elder sister and younger brother still talk so fondly about EVERY SINGLE day of their childhood spent growing up with such a brilliant and talented sister. They would, naturally, tell you this themselves . . . but sadly they were, er, unavailable for comment. Corinne CERTAINLY didn't put all her own dinner on to her sister's plate and make her eat it when her mum wasn't looking . . . and she CERTAINLY didn't dress up her younger brother in girls' clothes and call him Sarah. How dare you even suggest such a thing!

EL ASHFIELD is also the middle one of three (pure coincidence). Her sisters only have lovely things to say about her. Her little sister was certainly not forced to climb trees wearing her best dress, at the age of 5, in full view of the neighbours, nor was she left on the corner of the street when she fell off her bike. El certainly did not unfortunately kill her own cello by leaving it behind a reversing car, nor did she have any part in scaring the bejeezuz out of her elder sister with her habit of collecting spiders and leaving them to make webs on the ceiling - she is innocent!

www.trucilla.co.uk

Publisher: RAL Publications, UK: a subdivision of Rocket-Mind Publications Ltd.

CHAPTERS

1. THE PERFECT FAMILY (. . . OH, AND TRUCILLA!)
2. THE CACTUS MATTRESS
3. TRUCILLA SEEKS CASH (. . . ER, SORRY, TRUE LOVE)
4. I DO . . . ? (SERIOUSLY?)
5. A FROSTY RECEPTION
6. THE COUGHING COFFIN
7. THE PRISON BREAK BALLET
8. TARGET PRACTICE FOR BIRDS

READ ON TO FIND OUT, WHAT HAPPENED NEXT . . .

9 . EPILOGUE
10. CONFESSIONS

1

CHAPTER ONE

The
PERFECT FAMILY
(. . .OH, AND TRUCILLA)

Trucilla Applegate
was universally regarded
As lacking common decency,
good manners long discarded.
The eldest of four siblings, she was always in command
Of the others, who obeyed Trucilla's every least demand.

For next came Adriana,
who was such a gentle creature,
Then delicate Calista,
who resembled not one feature
Of Trucilla, with her tendencies to shout and be a slob.
(We must also give a mention to their younger brother, Bob.)

Their house had just three bedrooms but Trucilla didn't care,
She still demanded two of them and forced the rest to share.
She used one as a wardrobe, whilst her sisters shared a bed
And lack of space had prompted Bob to use the bath instead.

Their childhood was quite happy
when Trucilla wasn't there,
As when she was, she sat on them
or glued things to their hair.

In turn they kept a night-watch,
fully armed with bat and shield
Lest Trucilla should attack them,
whilst her presence was concealed.

Each Christmas time Trucilla set her own alarm for three,
Then tiptoed to her siblings' room as quietly as could be.
She would raid her sisters' stockings, taking out a gift or two,
Claiming Santa had run out and so had left an IOU.

Yes, living with Trucilla was a trial to be endured,
Psychologists were baffled
so she still remained uncured.
Her evil knew no bounds and it wasn't hard to tell
That both her parents (truth be told)
were scared of her as well.

Their mother ran a ballet class,
the siblings were so proud.
Well, all except Trucilla,
who was banned for 'being loud'.
She kicked and screamed and punched,
until sent home from all her classes.

No tutu ever fitted, and she broke one dancer's glasses!

And yet their mother hoped
they would desire a life of dance.
She stressed throughout their early years
the need for perfect stance.
Two sisters found a different trade,
Trucilla sought no job . . .
The only one who took it up professionally was Bob.

Poor Bob was half Trucilla's height
and less than half her girth.
He'd been the smallest sibling
ever since his early birth.
Though he was lean,
his limbs were strong from all his dancing training,
He'd still be on the disco floor when all around were waning.

Calista was a dainty child, most often to be found
With her head inside a cookbook
                    when her siblings weren't around.

She loved recipes and icing while Trucilla loved to eat . . .

To avoid her sister's anger, she would often bake a treat.

'These brownies are not big enough!'

Trucilla would complain

As Calista fled the kitchen and stood cowering in the rain.

'I asked for toffee slices!' spat Trucilla in a bait.

'You'll have to make some quickly –

come along, I will not wait!'

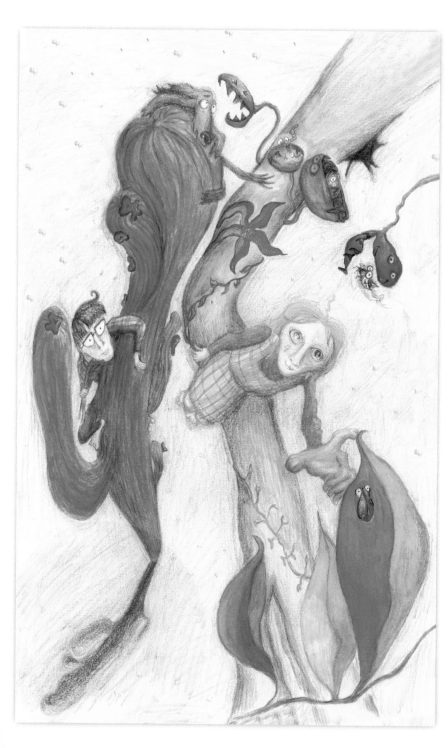

Trucilla bullied all the kids
(and teachers) at her school,
Unlike sweet Adriana who complied
with every rule.
Although she was a loner
she had one quite special friend,
. . . The only one Trucilla hadn't bothered to offend!

She saw him first, aged six,
inside his mother's flower shop.
They met beside a cactus,
as Vince peered over the top
At Adriana, standing there,
just fingering a leaf.
That someone else liked plants
as well came as a great relief!

They formed a special 'Gardening Club' but interest was small
And except its founder members no one ever joined at all!
But Vince and Adriana, well, they plainly didn't mind . . .
For now they had each other and the rest were not their kind.

2

CHAPTER TWO

THE
CACTUS MATTRESS

Their mother's death came suddenly,
and caused widespread upset.
(Her head cracked off a ceiling beam,
midway through pirouette!)
Calista mourned, Bob turned to dance
to help him with his pain,
While Adriana talked to plants
and gardened in the rain.

Trucilla, though, was strangely calm
and focused on their dad.
He questioned all her kindness,
thinking maybe she'd gone mad!
She made him soup, she cleaned the house
                         . . . and then was kinder still.
Trucilla offered to advise as he re-wrote his will!

Because she feared that at her father's tender stage of life
He might soon feel too lonely and seek out another wife,
Trucilla was 'concerned' that he might do something rash . . .
So courteously suggested she control the family cash!

Soon he was courting Betty,

　　　　　so her fears were not unfounded . . .

The lovers were quite smitten,

　　　　　their behaviour quite ungrounded!

'It's great news, Dad!' said Adriana

(who came out on top . . .

　. . . because Betty, she was Vince's mum,

　　　　　of Betty's Flower Shop.)

But Mr Applegate's demise came soon as, somewhat sadly,
A lovers' tiff upon a cliff had ended rather badly!
Trucilla caused an argument by stealing Betty's purse,
Then, when she left, Dad wrongly put his car . . . into reverse!

The other siblings couldn't speak for months,

such was the shock!
(Trucilla counted all the cash and bought a brand new frock.)
'For now I'm in control!' she said, triumphant and ecstatic.
Whilst others mourned,

Trucilla pawned the contents of the attic!

'Because I am so caring I've decided what to do,
I'll buy a cake and gardening shop . . .

and dance school . . . just for you!
I know I'm kind,' Trucilla said, 'but then of course I plan
To charge you double rent for those

. . . well, just because I can!'

She evicted all her siblings to the poky garden shed.
Bob slept on thorns and cacti as she hadn't left a bed!
His dancing was to suffer, as there simply wasn't space
For pirouette or plié with the plants around the place.

'It's just what Mum and Dad would want!'

a proud Trucilla smirked.

'I get these stressed out headaches

when I'm feeling overworked.

I'd be so good at many jobs – my apathy's a curse.
What can I do but loaf around with ever-bulging purse?'

'It's just not fair!' Bob said one night,

whilst tweezing out a thorn.

'Our childhood would have been so great

                    – if she had not been born!

We can't just leave

        – we've no spare cash through paying double rent.

Even if we clubbed together, we could scarce afford a tent!'

'Perhaps she's just misunderstood?' Calista would reply.

'For anyone to be this mean

                    – there must be reasons why.

But if we asked psychiatrists

                    I'm sure they'd merely say: "Maybe

It all stems back to some event when she was just a baby!"'

'That's right,' said Bob,

           'who knows what her behaviour really means?

Both Mum and Dad were lovely

            – we can't blame their dodgy genes!

And yet . . . ' he stammered,

           lying on the splintered wooden floor,

' . . . I'm rather scared for all of us.

           What might she have in store?'

3

CHAPTER THREE

TRUCILLA
SEEKS CASH
(ER, SORRY, TRUE LOVE)

Her siblings all worked round the clock –
Trucilla spent and spent,
On clothes and shoes and cars
. . . and, oh, a timeshare down in Kent.
And regularly she'd treat herself to makeovers or spas,
Then go and flaunt her 'look' in pricey restaurants and bars.

To no avail, however, as the men could not care less.
(And, truth be told,

these makeovers were not a great success!)
But still she made a CD called

'Watch out! I steal men's hearts!'
Which reached the giddy heights

of place three million in the charts.

'The internet's the way to go, I'll join a dating site . . . '
(She lied about her name, her job,

her age, her weight, her height!)
But still she got no interest, so thought it over-rated
Or guessed the men who read her profile felt intimidated!(?)
And yet Trucilla knew this cash just couldn't last for ever

For she had such expensive tastes

and compromised . . . well, never!

She thought of all her parents' conversations in the past:

'Trucilla needs a rich man, if her marriage is to last.'

Instead, Trucilla made a list of all the men in town,

Considering each name as she designed her wedding gown.
Calista could provide the cake, with Adriana's flowers . . .
And Bob would lead the dancing, as they partied on for hours.

Trucilla was convinced the men all thought her quite a catch,
She felt that they'd be honoured she'd consider them a match.
In her mind she was beautiful, so delicate and frail . . .
(On hearing of her plans,

               most men had tried to leave the Vale!)

Now Vince was always clever, and chose banking as his trade.
He'd made manager by thirty, so was also highly paid,
Though Adriana didn't give a stuff about his wealth,
But grew some anti-stress herbs

               in concern for Vincent's health.

'Your Vince must be quite rich,' Trucilla said one afternoon.
'D'ya think he wants to marry you? . . .

               D'ya think he'll ask you soon?'
'I hope so!' Adriana said. 'We've all been through so much.
And he bought me that allotment,

               which was a thoughtful touch!'
Trucilla hatched an evil plot to steal her sister's man.

(Though truth be told it wasn't a sophisticated plan!)
She got Vince drunk one evening

on the local farmer's brew . . .

Then made him sign a contract as he staggered from the loo.

'Oh, no! Poor Adriana!' yelped Calista when she heard.
'And Vince, he's signed a contract . . .

so he's given her his word!

He's bound to go ahead with it . . . Trucilla must be stopped!'
While Bob just stood there speechless with his jaw still fully

dropped.

'It's so unfair!'
said Adriana,
hearing the bad
news.
'She knows he
cannot tolerate
those potent
farmer's brews!

She got him drunk deliberately, of that you can be sure.
She won't maintain his garden . . .

and she'll spend until he's poor!'

'It's time she learned a lesson!' said Calista, with a wince.
'She might get everything she wants . . .

but she's not getting Vince!
He's Adriana's boyfriend . . . I'll do everything I can
To put a stop to this – Trucilla's latest evil plan!'

4
CHAPTER FOUR

I DO . . . ?
(SERIOUSLY?)

The engagement was announced, and Vince's mum
collapsed in shock.
In case Trucilla moved in,
Betty changed her bedroom lock!
Two weeks before the wedding
she gave Vince one final chance
To call it off . . . he didn't . . . so she disappeared to France!

Vince grew to love Trucilla, or so he'd been informed.
He was busy one day, ironing, when in Trucilla stormed.
'Well, are we getting married soon or what?'

her voice demanded,
And from that day poor Vincent knew

his dance card had been branded.

Now he stood bewildered as a mournful groom-to-be,
Viewing the congregation with a silent, wordless plea.
He felt that, if there was a God, someone would intervene . . .
To prevent this fearsome union on which he wasn't keen!

The seconds ticked, he mopped his brow

and straightened his bow tie . . .
Acknowledging he stood there, but still contemplating why.

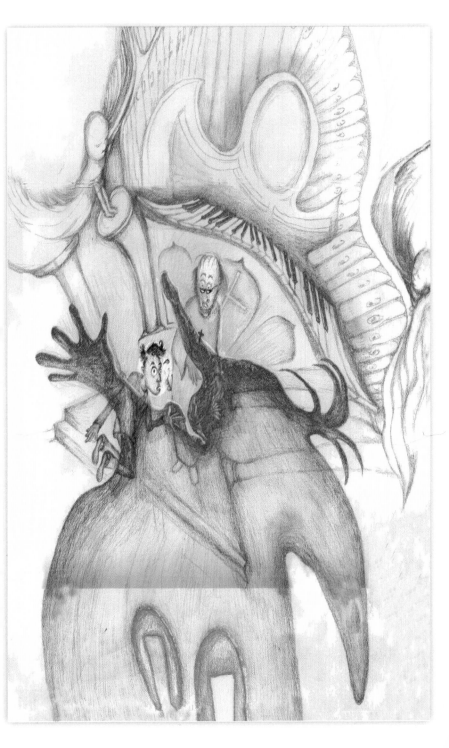

And if he ran . . . would that be rude . . .

        and would Trucilla mind?

For despite her reputation,

        she just might (this once) be kind.

In the absence of her father, few desired to take his place
To escort Trucilla down the aisle in all her pomp and grace.
Eventually she opted for the safest bet, poor Bob,
And caught short with no excuses, he'd agreed to do the job.

'You're gripping me too tightly!'

        winced young Bob as he turned blue.

'KEEP WALKING!'

        boomed Trucilla, while he mouthed,

        'I'm trying to!'

'Just look how happy Vincent is!'

        Trucilla glimpsed her groom,

As he writhed and winced and sweated

        and prepared to meet his doom.

The organ chimed,

        poor Vincent groaned,

        the Vicar looked uneasy,

Trucilla in her wedding dress made even him feel queasy!

He knew it wasn't right,

but felt (this once) it would be fine . . .

If he quickly slipped poor Vincent

just a small communion wine.

The Vicar started cautiously, surveying those collected,

A headcount of just six was still six more than he'd expected!
Trucilla was despised (although the numbers would be higher
If she hadn't just insulted the entire parish choir!)

But close outside, a darkened figure loitered near a grave.
The Applegates both rested 'neath their tombstone,
'Clive and Maeve'.
The grass was neat and freshly cut,
the tombstone nicely dusted.
The flowerpot had been replaced,
the old one having rusted.

'IT'S TIME,' the darkened figure mouthed,
'FOR ME TO INTERVENE!'
(A shrouded face and jet black hood
ensured they'd not be seen.)
'It's YOUR fault that it's come to this!'
the darkened figure wailed,
As it ripped the invitation that Trucilla kindly mailed.

'I OBJECT!'
the figure shouted,
as it flew into the church.

'She's fat, she's rude, she's mean

        . . . and once she killed my winning birch!'
'You're too late, Adriana,'

        the poor Vicar whispered back.
She checked her watch and noticed

        all the crowd were dressed in black.

'Whoopsy!' Adriana said. 'I'm sorry for your loss.
I thought this was my sister's wedding – that's why I was cross,
She isn't very nice, you see, but now is not the time
For me to share the details of her every petty crime!'

        'I stalled as long as possible!' the Vicar then replied.
    'I asked them to object ten times . . . and even tried to hide
        So they couldn't say their vows, you see,
          but she still found me out.
          They left as man and wife, my dear,
          the groom still drenched in doubt!'

And cursing that her watch had stopped, poor Adriana left.
(Being mid-way through a funeral, the Vicar thought it best!)
'It's not too late!' she cried out as she stole his waiting car.
'Plan B it has to be . . . for the reception can't be far!'

5

CHAPTER FIVE

A

FROSTY RECEPTION

'And now I'll do my speeches,
whilst we start to cut the cake!'
Trucilla glared at Bob,
who was by that stage just awake.
The bride and groom stood, knife in hand,
Vince looking terrified . . .
As Trucilla took a tier herself, then tossed the rest aside.

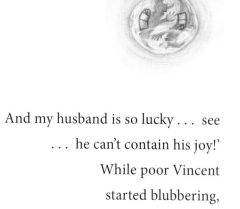

'I hate
to sound immodest,
but I think
you'll all agree
That you've never seen
a blushing bride
as beautiful as me!

And my husband is so lucky . . . see
. . . he can't contain his joy!'
While poor Vincent
started blubbering,
the poor, remorseful boy.

'She's taken the whole bottom tier . . . she'll never eat all that!'
'Trucilla?' Bob replied. 'She's never cared if she gets fat!'
'But she must eat the *top* tier . . . it's made 'specially for her!'
As Calista watched uneasily, her guilt began to stir.

'You came then, Adriana!'
Bob announced in great delight.
'I'm in disguise . . . be quiet . . . you didn't see me here tonight!'

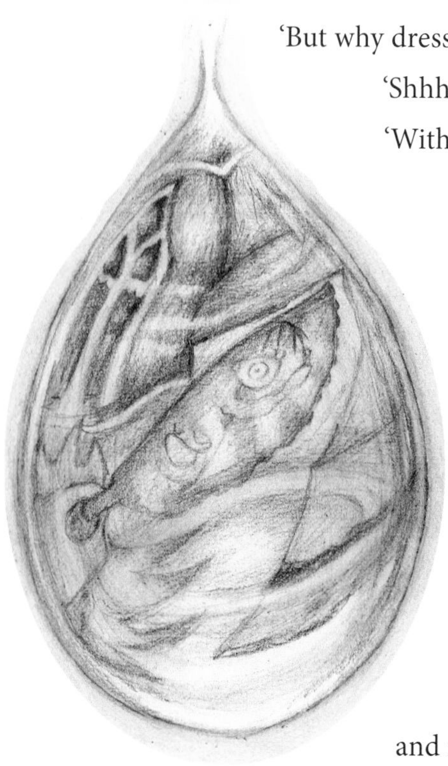

'But why dress up like that?' he asked.
'Shhh, Bob!' her voice replied.
'With you all draped in black,'
he laughed,
'they'll think someone
has died!'

'A quick word,
Adriana!'
And Calista
took her arm.
Adriana saw
her face a-glow
and felt her moistened palm.
'Just do not touch
the wedding cake . . . be sure to tell Bob too!
I plan to kill a sibling here . . . but neither one of you!'

'You put poison in the cake?' Poor Adriana's stomach stirred,
And they spoke a little softer, lest they should be overheard.
'Well, only in the upper tier – the rest of it is fine!'

'I'm afraid the middle isn't . . . for in that tier I put mine!'
'You tried to poison Trucey, too?' Calista said in shock
As waitresses stood staring at the bulging bridal frock
While it whirled around the dance floor with a startled
Vince in tow. . .
Well, until he got his neck caught in one understated
bow!

'That's why I'm here.
I spiked the mix,
when no one
else could
see . . .

It's
amazing
what you
learn
 in twenty
years
of
botany!

And you?
Of course,
you baked it!'
Adriana saw it all
As they glanced,
concerned, towards
the cake across the
dining hall.

'The middle tier is

missing. QUICK! It
really must be found.'
But Calista stood
and watched Trucilla
whirling Vince
around.
And in her left hand
. . . what was that?
Calista gulped
in fear,
As Trucilla

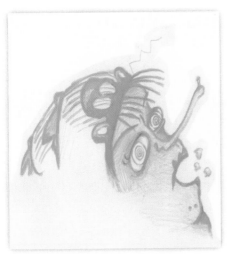

tried to feed
poor Vince
the poisoned middle
tier.

'Nooooo!' screamed
Adriana, whipping off
her balaclava

As the waitresses all gathered round, amused at the palaver.

'Don't eat it,
Vince . . .
DON'T EAT IT!'
Adriana's plea
rang out,
As Bob
pirouetted,
wondering
what the fuss
was all about.

. . . the siblings watched in awe . . .

As their bossy elder sister choked and crumpled to the floor.

'IT'S THEM . . . IT MUST HAVE . . . BEEN!'

were Trucilla's last known words.

(There were

other stifled mutterings,

but none that could be heard!)

. . . after an embarrassingly brief pause . . .

'Well, never mind!' said Bob.
'It's true . . . we all must die some day,'

As he checked the DJ's music for a ballet track to play.

'Yes, she'd want us to be happy!'
said Calista with a wink,

                    Whilst Adriana checked her pulse
                         and quickly tried to think.

'Keep quiet, Adriana!'
said Calista.
'Who will know
That we ever tried to kill her? . . .
It is such a lucky blow!
Despite our best attempts
            they'll say she choked,
                   it's just a fact!'

And Adriana nodded, seeing one tier still intact . . .

'IT'S MURDER! Call the police!'

a waitress shouted, overhearing,
As crowds had formed around the corpse,

where Bob was busy jeering.
'Who said anything of poison? . . .

No, I'm sure it's just a choking!'
'That was me!' said Adriana. But with hindsight I was joking!'

'It's nothing, miss, to laugh about! Now I must analyse
The remainder of this wedding cake . . .

and why you're in disguise!
It looks as though your answers might need

further contemplation
So once you've made them up, why don't you tell us . . .

down the station?'

'But you can't prove a thing!' poor Adriana stuttered back –
Until they found her diagrams detailing the attack.
'My plan to kill Trucilla' was the header of each page.
'Is there more you'd like to tell us?'

asked the policeman. 'At this stage?'

'A small piece of advice, miss,'

said the DCI, amused.

'Next time don't confess to murder . . .

not until you've been accused!'

Calista wondered if next time

she shouldn't write things down

As news about the sisters' antics spread around the town.

6

CHAPTER SIX

THE
COUGHING COFFIN

'So let's just get this straight,'
the DCI said, sipping tea,
'You heard about this plant
through your research in botany,
And knew it was so potent that the very smallest speck
Once reduced a crash of rhinos to a blubbering, legless wreck?'

'That's right!' said Adriana. 'And although, of course, I know
That what I did was very wrong – I thought it worth a go.
Trucilla was a meanie, she was famed for being vile,
And so I knew my grief would only last the briefest while.'

Next door Calista too was not denying her intention
To polish off Trucilla through her culinary invention.
'It might be rather dull but I used arsenic, that's all.
In fact, I'm quite offended my tier wasn't touched at all!'

And so within a tiny cell, inside the village jail,
Both sisters sat awaiting trial – too penniless for bail.
And Vince would visit every day and often stayed for hours
(Due to visiting restrictions he'd bring photos of their flowers.)

The Thursday of the funeral the sisters were permitted
To both attend and say goodbye.
                              (Their teeth were fully gritted!)
But, as in life, Trucilla was to have the final word
For as the coffin headed south, a spluttering could be heard. . .

'IT'S ME, TRUCILLA! LET ME OUT! IT'S TRUE – I'M

STILL ALIVE!

My sisters tried to kill me – but I knew that I'd survive

To tell the TV channels all about my tragic story.

Now every paper will rejoice. . .

I'M BACK IN ALL MY GLORY!'

'No way!' Bob muttered to himself. 'Please tell me it's not true?

I should have known. . . I should have guessed. . . there's just one person who

Has a stomach made of iron and is able to digest

A heavy-duty poison that's laid animals to rest!'

'Well, goodness me!' the Vicar cried. 'I've not seen this before!'

Observing that the prison guards had fainted on the floor.

(And just this once, to calm his nerves, he felt it would be fine

To quickly slip himself a very small communion wine.)

'That's it!. . . We're free!. . . She's still alive!. . . WE'RE FREE!'

Calista said.

'Oh, not so fast!' Trucilla smirked. 'I think you'll find instead

That though the outcome may have changed, intent remained the same.'

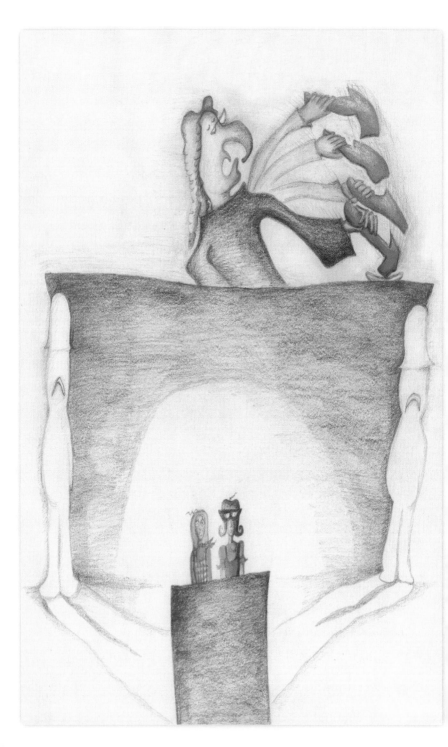

They were thrown back into prison as Bob wept, 'It's such a
shame!'

'I've met Trucilla,' said the judge, 'and so I understand
The cruelty and bullying that must have forced your hand.
With deep regret, I sentence both to serve out seven years!'
The court collapsed in tears and boos (above Trucilla's cheers!)

And just outside the courtroom,
all the world's press had descended,
The siblings branded 'martyrs',
which was not what they'd intended.
'FREE THE APPLEGATES!' 'THEY WERE PROVOKED!'
the banners stated.
Trucilla had the worldwide fame
she'd always thought she rated.

But down a quiet corridor, far from the prying mob
Stood Vince in deep discussion
with a shell-shocked, angry Bob.
'I'm sorry, Vince, it's come to this –
but I know you will agree
That this is what we'll have to do to set my sisters free. . .'

7

CHAPTER SEVEN

THE
PRISON BREAK
BALLET

With many months of planning
over pots of tea and cake
Our heroes Bob and Vincent
slowly planned the prison break.
Their outfits had been purchased –
there was nothing left to chance.
They'd even spent months practising
a special ballet dance.

Could anyone have guessed when Bob
would visit his relations
That he and Vince were making plans
so far above their stations?
Their first stop Adriana, who could help them from the start
By slipping notes of dosage for a tranquillising dart.

Though Adriana also had a second part to play:
With subtle hand manoeuvres
when the guards would glance away
She now advised (with hindsight
and what happened to Trucilla)

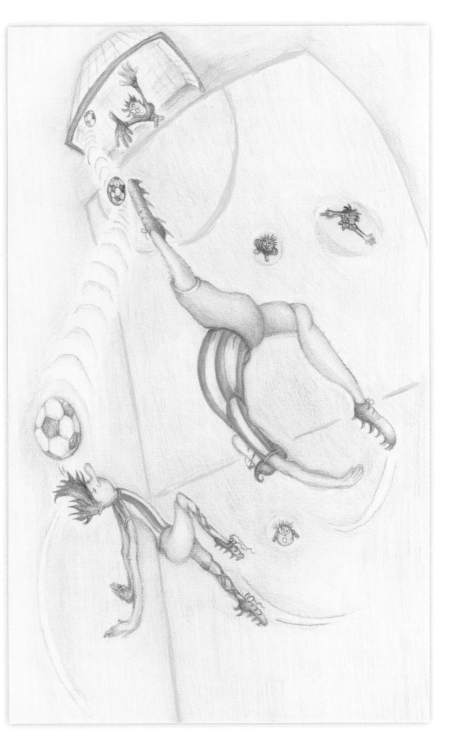

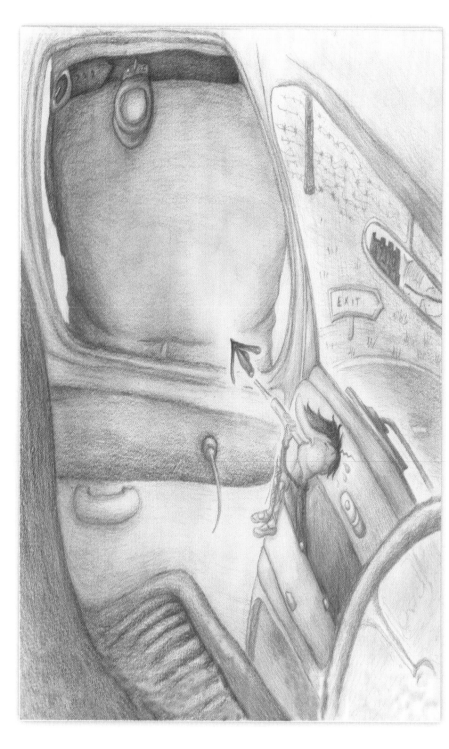

Exactly how much of a dose to mix with the vanilla.

Calista then took over to ensure there weren't mistakes
When Bob and Vince were mixing up

their special fairy cakes.
Advising on ingredients and icing patterns too
And slipping them cake cases

when the guards were in the loo.

So everything was now in place

– our heroes could proceed.
They triple-checked the kit for every little thing they'd need.
(Indeed the judge had mentioned

when he had the sisters booked
That 'If they happened to escape. . . it might be overlooked.')

Bob drove up to the prison gates

and knew the time had come.
(A hidden Vince fired two darts

at the first guard's ample bum.)

A third dart quickly silenced one patrolling by the fence,
A fourth and fifth and sixth required

                      – his partner was immense!

And so the boys (in costume) once inside the prison doors
Were ushered to the dining hall and met with huge applause.
One guard then introduced them:
'Ladies, how's this for a treat?
It's Robert and Vincentia, with their stunning ballet feet!'

The show commenced with 'Oooohs' and 'Aaaahs'

                      of genuine surprise
That Bob could look so graceful with a partner twice his size.
The crowd were mesmerised by every leap across the floor,
And many were convinced they'd seen them on TV before.

Then as the show concluded
with a curtain call. . . or seven,
The general consensus:
these were dancers
sent from heaven!

And Vince had to deliver he performance of his life
When one inmate enquired if the pair were man and wife.

'We're glad that you enjoyed the show!'

                        said Bob, still bathed in sweat.

'And happier to tell you that it isn't over yet.

You were a lovely audience

                        and so, please, if you can,

Do join us now for tea and scones.'

                        (The next part of the plan!)

And only minutes later, any idiot could tell
Calista's special fairy cakes had gone down rather well
As all the inmates and the guards

                        were sleeping side by side.

Except, of course, the Applegates

                        – all giggling with pride.

'COME ON! LET'S GO!' Bob shouted.

                        'This sedation won't last long!

We can't give them a double dose,

as that would be plain wrong!

'JUST DRIVE!' said Vince,

though Adriana thought it might be groovy

Being smuggled out in laundry

– as she'd seen it in a movie!

So, in a blaze of glory, our quartet drove through the gates
Away from sleeping prison guards and hundreds of inmates.
But being so responsible, young Bob still found the time
To shut the gates behind them. (Not to add to local crime!)

You might think that our tale ends there

– though you would be mistaken –

As after all brave Bob and Vince

had saved the sisters' bacon.

But just before you close your book,

I do suggest you wait

For if you turn the page

– you'll find there's more in Chapter Eight.

8

CHAPTER EIGHT

TARGET PRACTICE

For Birds

So safely back at home,
each with cocoa, jam and toast,
The sisters sat reflecting
over which part hurt the most.
Trucilla had their cash, but this was nothing really since
She wasn't just alive but, worse, was married to poor Vince!

'I used to live my life in quite a pleasant, moral manner,
But look what I've become NOW!' said a woeful Adriana.
'You're still my special gardening love,'

said Vincent with assurance.
'Though if I'm still HER husband,

I might take out life insurance!'

'There must be something else

that can be done about our sister,
She can't get clean away with this!' began a sad Calista.
'I'VE GOT IT!' Adriana screamed (Bob started to applaud).
'For if I'm not mistaken she is guilty too – of FRAUD!

'Before she married Vince, she formed a club to find a man,
I once remember seeing her official business plan.
She charged those men a fortune,

just to join, despite their looks,
Because she claimed that "royalty and celebs"

were on her books!'

Calista smiled. 'I'll phone the Fraud Squad now

and dob her in!'
'Before you do. . . ' said Adriana, with a gentle grin,
'. . . I know the police are turning a blind eye to our escape,
But we should not be witnesses – just think of the red tape!'

'That's right!' said Bob.

'I'll do it, yes, the pleasure is all mine!
I hope she'll get a sentence, or a very hefty fine.'
True to his word he told them all about it the next day,
Then all Trucilla's business files

were promptly snatched away.

The same judge smirked: 'Miss Applegate. . .

                              I've heard that name before.

Despite your newfound status, you are NOT above the law.

I hear you've never had a job – what fun it's going to be,

Three hundred hours of service in your own community!'

Trucilla, though, had never done a day's work in her life

So hence the plan to marry well and be a pampered wife.

Don't laugh but here's the irony, for on her first full day

The shock of work was all too much

                              – she dropped dead anyway!

Which left, of course, our Vincent as a widower once more.

But this time at the funeral there were no shocks in store.

Vince gave it just one day

                              – to double-check he'd be composed,

Then promptly got down on one knee and finally proposed!

When Adriana married Vince,

                              the church was swamped in flowers.

The Vicar was so tearful, the service lasted hours.
(And after all they'd been through,

                        felt this once it would be fine
If he slipped the congregation

                  just a small communion wine!)

And yet, there's one last twist before we all say our goodbyes.
The siblings went to hear the will – and left with heavy sighs.
Trucilla thought she'd dedicate her money to the friends
And family she'd tortured. Was this a bid to make amends?

Well, no. . . her final wish: for statues placed all over town
Where, from a height, Trucilla could be always looking down
On those whose lives she'd ruined,

                  or on those she'd always hated.
For her to be immortal, yes, she'd always thought it fated!

Whenever they were passing through,

                 the siblings always stopped
For a photo with Trucilla where the bird poo often dropped.
Their sister had the last laugh though

                 – the last part of her will
Insisted that her home town be renamed 'Trucilla-Ville'.

END

THE END

YOU'RE SURE THIS TIME? IT'S

THE END

SHE'S NOT COMING BACK
AGAIN, IS SHE?

9
CHAPTER NINE

THE
EPILOGUE
(WHAT HAPPENED NEXT)

FIVE YEARS ON . . . THE INTERVIEW

Well, a massive hello to you all from Trucilla-Ville, home of the famed Applegate sisters (and Bob). My name is Wannabee Huge, talented local reporter and television presenter, and I'm here today to EXCLUSIVELY interview the Applegate sisters (and Bob) five years on from the international coverage of the Trucilla scandal. I'll be asking them REALLY probing questions about what they've been up to since and how they have coped with the pressure. My show will be aired by Media Channel NotReallyNews next year, but here (for you special readers only) is a sneak preview of those in-depth interviews . . .

So, Adriana, talk us through the last five years since you hit the headlines?
ADRIANA: After Vince and I got married we set up our new home at Cheeseweed Cottage. The following year we were blessed with the arrival of our twins: Coriander Dandelion and Nettles Asparagus. (We couldn't believe it on Coriander's first day at nursery when she met another Coriander in her class. . . what were the odds?)
Indeed. Do you still run the flower shop?
Yes, we're very busy – constantly entering competitions and doing weddings, parties and things.
Do you enjoy creating wedding displays because it reminds you of your special day with Vince? Or, can I ask, do you find doing funeral flowers hard because it brings back sad memories of Trucilla?
I loved doing the flowers as it was such a special occasion and you could see the smiling faces on all the guests. . . it was such a happy day.
[ADRIANA TAKES A MOMENT, CLEARLY LOST IN JOYOUS MEMORIES.]
Er, for your wedding, yes. . . But I meant for Trucilla's funeral?
I WAS talking about Trucilla's funeral.
OK. . . Do you hope for a larger family one day, being one of four yourself?
Well, in fact, I'm expecting another baby in the spring. A boy! We're toying with the name Parsley Manure but we'd hate there to be someone else in his class with the same name. I would love to let you be first to

see a photo of him, but we've sold the rights to a popular magazine and then we'll donate all the proceeds to our favourite charity.

Adriana, it was lovely catching up with you, Vince, Coriander ,and Nettles. . .

. . . and our dog, Sneezewort!

Ah, yes, of course. *Though I'm afraid I think he might have piddled on your...*

Yes, he did. So, best of luck. . . and of course also with your charity helpline: Forgive a sibling. . . don't just try to poison them.

Many thanks. It's a catchy name, isn't it? But Calista is the founder, so I'll let her tell you more about it.

Many thanks, Adriana. Well, Bob, how lovely to see you. . . and what an entrance! Now, I hear you've become something of a hero and a pin-up in these parts?

BOB: Many thanks. I always like to dance into a room – it gives off positive energy, I find. Yes, a pin-up, that's right. I've even become the face of Ballet Tights Weekly. . . who would have thought it possible!

Hmmm. So, five years on, Bob, do you still find you think about Trucilla every day, or have you been able. . . in some small way. . . to move on and find peace?

Who?

Trucilla. Trucilla? Your ex-big-sister?

[BOB TAKES A MOMENT]

81

Oh, yes, sorry. No, I've managed to block it all out rather well. . . except for those annoying statues! They're always covered in bird poo, you know. Don't know why the council can't take them down myself.

Right.

I mean, we're talking over one hundred poos a day sometimes, it's. . .

So, moving on! It's great that you were able to turn all this into something positive.

I actually created a Forgiveness Dance at the time, which obviously helped. Would you like to see it?

NO, REALLY! . . . I mean, maybe. . . later.

OK.

So, you still run your dance school? My goodness, what a busy man you must be.

That's right. I've even got assistants. Two of them used to be prison guards, but they were so moved by my dance performance with Vince that day, they re-trained and now even teach point-work. Beautiful lines, they have!

Lovely. And any romance in your life, Bob?

No, not at the moment. I'm far too busy for any of that. I went out for dinner with a lady last month, but she was awfully bossy and rather greedy too. . . ordered five starters and three bottles of wine straight away, so we didn't really hit it off. She reminded me of someone but I couldn't think who. . .

Er. . . Trucilla?

Ah, yes. Now you mention it, that's who it was. It's been bugging me ever since!

Thanks, Bob, great catching up with you. So, Calista. I've already seen how well your brother and sister are doing and how surprisingly unaffected they seem by --
CALISTA: Do you smell burning?
[Twenty-five minutes later Wannabee begins to worry if this has all been too painful for Calista. Has revisiting these horrible memories and emotions been too much for her? Has she. . .]
Good news! The Knitting Club's Victoria sandwich lives on. . . Stand down, Fire Brigade!
Oh. . . great. Er, did you say Fire Brigade?
No, no, slip of the tongue. Where were we, Wannabee?
So, the baking business is clearly still going strong. To what do you

attribute your success?
Organisation. I'm an extremely organised person, as you can see.
Hmmm. . . Of course. Is it true you were considered as one of the possible bakers for the Queen's Diamond Jubilee cake?
Yes, that's right. Only sadly I missed that email and didn't hear the answer-machine messages in time. I had been forced to move out due to a tiny little house-fire incident!
Oh, what a shame. Well, anyway, do you find that, five years on, you. . . er, can you hear crying?
HECK! Is that my daughter or the cat? I forget where I

left either of them when distracted by –
Painful memories of Trucilla?
– a really good recipe on the telly!
Right. . . How nice, a baby girl. Let me guess what her name is. . . Vanilla Demerara Free-Range?
Oh, Adriana told you! It's lovely, isn't it? Unusual.
What?. . . I was RIGHT? Yes. . . it's lovely. So, anyway, you still find time to run your new helpline?
Yes, we basically offer positive support and discuss ways of working towards forgiving siblings, rather than just poisoning them. We have a Forgiveness Song actually, it goes like. . .
Lovely. And is the charity doing well?
Really well. Lots of support out there. I'd show you the business accounts and new posters but. . .
They went up in the house fire, I suppose?
Yes.
Thanks, Calista.
[THE VICAR ENTERS - THE ONLY INTERVIEWEE TO DEMAND HIS HAIR AND MAKE-UP IS DONE FOR THE CAMERA.]
Well, thank you so much for agreeing to meet us today. . . eventually.
VICAR: You are most welcome, of course. Is this my best side?
We promise not to make any 'More tea, Vicar?' jokes!
Yes, well, frankly SOME tea would be a start. Not even a custard cream in sight! Just this fancy fizzy water stuff. Joan Higglebottom makes fresh scones and jam when I come round, you know!
Oh, sorry. Anyway, we're here to discuss the Applegates and how they are all faring five years on.
Well, I christened Coriander, Nettles and Vanilla, so I'm still in regular contact with the family.
It must have been lovely, to see them moving on from such a hard time?
Yes. WEIRD names though, aren't they? What's wrong with Jane? I say. Or a simple Thomas? . . . Off the record, I had to slip myself a very small communion wine, just to keep a straight face! I blame all those celebrities for this new trend. Think of the poor Vicars, I say! Anyway, Miss. . . er?

Wannabee.
[WE PAUSE THE INTERVIEW FOR A MOMENT AFTER THE
VICAR SNORTS HIS FIZZY WATER THE WRONG WAY.]
**Do you think the community on the whole has come to terms with what
happened to Trucilla and with her sisters' behaviour at the time? Or are
they perhaps still––**
Yes.
Oh, right. Anything further to add to that?
*Well, you know that Calista and Adriana have set up this charity to
help others in the same boat? I helped with the lyrics of the Forgiveness
Song. Have you heard it? There was talk of a chart release and a tour
supporting some boy band, but I didn't have the time this year. It goes
like this. . .*
NO! Well, maybe later.
*Bob has created a Forgiveness Dance too. Bless. There's even talk of
Trucilla the Musical, you know?*
We did hear something about that, yes.
*I'm in two minds about it myself. I mean, I don't think we should
be celebrating the life of someone mean or the terrible thing that the
Applegate sisters tried to do. Then again, they were provoked and the
stage show would be focusing
mainly on forgiveness, which is
more my thing. . . plus I can't help
wondering who might play me if it
goes to DVD! Though obviously I
turned down the panto offer.*

**Oh, actually one last quick
question. As you clearly believe
in the after-life, do you think
Trucilla might still be hanging
around somewhere out there and
her ghost might be planning her
revenge?**
[THE VICAR HAS FAINTED.]

10

CHAPTER TEN

CONFESSIONS

SPECIAL MESSAGE FROM THE AUTHOR

Well, hello, readers. . . Corinne the author here. You know, it's always nice to have a bit of banter with the readers of your books and to get them involved in some way. So, one morning it came to me. . . I needed to discover what crimes YOU readers might have committed towards a sibling or family member – and, frankly, my enquiries have produced some truly shocking results! From Wales to Australia, and covering all age brackets, the sordid tales came flooding in.

Might I say what a very mean lot you are? (No offence!) Some have shouldered their guilt in secrecy for many years, so in order to allow them to move on finally, I have rated their crime on my Mean-O-Meter and then passed sentence, which is required before we can all sing the Forgiveness Song together. I must stress. . . PLEASE do not try to replicate any of these crimes at home! Some of them are truly hideous, and I may require further therapy in order to come to terms with hearing about them!

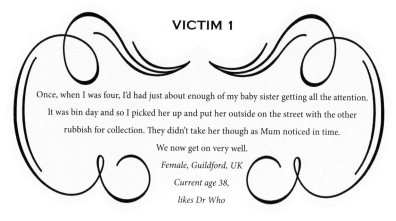

VICTIM 1

Once, when I was four, I'd had just about enough of my baby sister getting all the attention. It was bin day and so I picked her up and put her outside on the street with the other rubbish for collection. They didn't take her though as Mum noticed in time.

We now get on very well.

Female, Guildford, UK

Current age 38,

likes Dr Who

Corinne says: Oooh, now that's REALLY mean. If I were your younger sister I'm not entirely sure I'd trust you ever again at family gatherings. I'm sure putting the bins out every week must bring back some horrifying memories for her. Just hearing the bin lorry must bring on palpitations. It's good that you confessed this though. . . 34 YEARS LATE, but still good!

Mean-o-Meter Rating: 9/10

Sentenced to: You like bins? Volunteer to help your local refuse collection by cleaning out wheelie bins for a month. That's right – you need to personally remove every snotty tissue, toe-nail clipping or fish skin that has been left welded to the side for years, commencing at 4.30 a.m. each morning. YES, UNPAID!. . . NEXT!

VICTIM 2

Once I was watching this really funny film and I didn't want to stop the DVD to go to the toilet, and I was laughing so much I weed on the carpet. I told Mummy it was our dog.

Female, Cardiff, Wales

Aged 6,

likes all purple things

Corinne: Oh, yes, the old 'blame the family pet' ploy – shame on you! I do hope your mum or dad didn't tell the dog off too forcefully or make them wear pull-up training pants for a crime YOU committed!

Mean-o-Meter Rating: 8/10

(It would have been 7/10, but I'm particularly harsh on animal-framing!)

Sentence: So that your dog knows you are TRULY sorry for your terrible crime, you must switch beds for the week. The dog will be extremely comfortable under your (no doubt) purple and flowery duvet while you sleep scrunched up in his bed on the kitchen floor. Furthermore I want you to have a t-shirt printed, stating 'It wasn't the Dog. . . IT WAS ME!', which must also be worn daily throughout your sentence. I do hope the film was worth it! . . . NEXT!

VICTIM 3

Once I took my big brother's pencil without asking, but gave it back later.

Male, Cork, Ireland

Aged 7,

likes The Avengers and carrot cake

CONFESSIONS

Corinne: Please don't waste my time!   *Mean-o-Meter Rating: 0.5/10*

Sentence: You are clearly a lovely chap with no place among such criminals as these. I suggest you go out and do something just slightly naughty soon (perhaps jump in some mud or burp after a fizzy drink), or else you might be storing up all your naughtiness for later in life, and I genuinely fear you might explode!. . . NEXT!

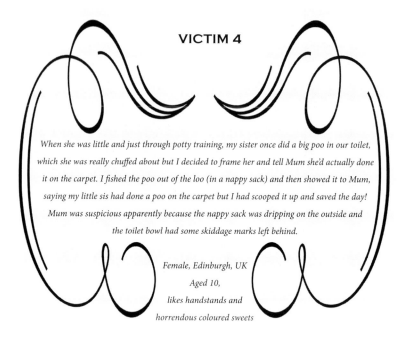

VICTIM 4

When she was little and just through potty training, my sister once did a big poo in our toilet, which she was really chuffed about but I decided to frame her and tell Mum she'd actually done it on the carpet. I fished the poo out of the loo (in a nappy sack) and then showed it to Mum, saying my little sis had done a poo on the carpet but I had scooped it up and saved the day! Mum was suspicious apparently because the nappy sack was dripping on the outside and the toilet bowl had some skiddage marks left behind.

Female, Edinburgh, UK
Aged 10,
likes handstands and
horrendous coloured sweets

Corinne: Ah-ha, I knew it was only a matter of time before a poo- or toilet-related incident was brought to my attention! I should state that I was forced to read this confession TWICE such was the severity of the crime, to ensure that I had my poo-pilfering facts straight. I have heard of siblings stealing many things from each other before but never a poo. I might have to lie down!

Mean-O-Meter Rating: 10.5/10

Sentence: Well. . . where to begin? Each year for your birthday your sister must give you a poo-related gift. I'm not talking about whoopy cushions or stink bombs. . . no, I'm thinking about poo-shaped jewellery, ornaments, or even a nice jumper emblazoned with an artist's impression of THAT POO, to remind you never to indulge in poo-crime ever again. Each gift must be worn with pride for at least a week, alongside a sandwich board stating: 'KEEP YOUR DISTANCE – I STEAL POO!' for the duration of the sentence. Er, NEXT. . . I think!

VICTIM 5

When I was a little boy, my sister ALWAYS used to dress me up in girls' clothes and tell me that I was actually a little girl called Sarah and she. . .

Corinne: Apologies for that interruption, everyone. Yes, OK, little brother, it was a looong time ago, so get over it, man! (Ironically he did go on to marry a lovely girl named Sarah, but that's by the by.) On to some more worthy cases. Has anyone else noticed there has been a trend for mean big sister stories, rather than mean big brother ones? Oh, no, hang on, I'm about to take that back apparently. . . NEXT!

VICTIM 6

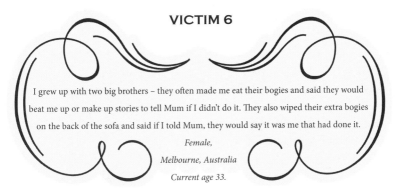

I grew up with two big brothers – they often made me eat their bogies and said they would beat me up or make up stories to tell Mum if I didn't do it. They also wiped their extra bogies on the back of the sofa and said if I told Mum, they would say it was me that had done it.

Female,
Melbourne, Australia
Current age 33.

91

CONFESSIONS

Corinne: Well, call me a softie, but your story made me want to weep. How you must have suffered! I can only imagine that television adverts for nasal sprays must still make you very nervous, and bring it all back to you. Nasal crime is, again, one of the worst there is and something I take very seriously. I'm so glad you finally summoned up the courage to share your tragic tale with us, my friend.   *Mean-O-Meter Rating: 11/10*
(Due to the sustained nature of your torment I felt an extra 0.5 should be awarded over the tragic poo story.)

Sentence: You mention in the rest of your letter that you now have children of your own. I'm so happy that you have been able to move on with your life in this way. Obviously I recommend focusing on FORGIVENESS rather than purely REVENGE attacks, but should your children happen to be suffering from snotty noses whilst at their uncles' houses, I recommend pointing them in the direction of the sofa! You also mentioned one brother was due to get married soon. Perhaps 'sharing' this story with both the bride and the best man may be wise, and it will certainly prompt his new bride to double-check her white frock and veil at regular intervals. Old habits do die hard after all! Clearly should you ever be entertaining your brothers at a dinner party or for Christmas dinner and 'happen' to sneeze into their food, this fact could easily be overlooked. No need to tell them!

VICTIM 7

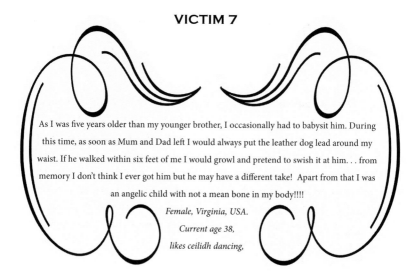

As I was five years older than my younger brother, I occasionally had to babysit him. During this time, as soon as Mum and Dad left I would always put the leather dog lead around my waist. If he walked within six feet of me I would growl and pretend to swish it at him. . . from memory I don't think I ever got him but he may have a different take! Apart from that I was an angelic child with not a mean bone in my body!!!!

Female, Virginia, USA.
Current age 38,
likes ceilidh dancing,

Corinne: Not a mean bone in your body, eh? I think I will be the judge of that!

Mean-O-Meter Rating: 8/10

Sentence: What is this trend of involving canines in sibling feuds? Well, as you seem to enjoy pretending to be an animal so much, try this on for size! I have booked you a slot to appear as the back end of Daisy the Cow this Christmas panto season. Sadly the pantomime is here in Edinburgh so that's going to cost you a bit on flights! Equally sadly, I am reliably informed that the gentleman who will be playing the front of the cow is very fond of beans on toast for lunch, prior to performances. Enjoy. NEXT!. . .

VICTIM 8

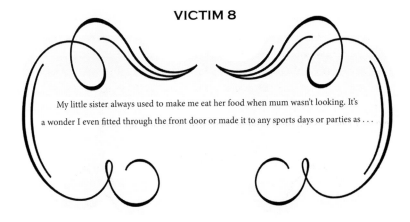

My little sister always used to make me eat her food when mum wasn't looking. It's a wonder I even fitted through the front door or made it to any sports days or parties as . . .

Corinne: Oh for goodness sake! How did that make it into the book? I paid for hundreds of hours of therapy for you, big sis, so please can we finally let this go and could you both stop interrupting me. Besides, the hours of compulsory board games you made me play each Christmas day were revenge enough, surely. I respectfully ask that you both go away as some of us are trying to work here. Advising victims from around the world on such matters is a very serious business! Oh, and don't even THINK about bringing up the time that the gerbil escaped and you both thought I'd cooked it in mum's birthday cake that year. The timing was purely coincidental. Apologies everyone, where was I? Indeed, perhaps I should have a final lie down with smelling salts before our final confession. It doesn't half take it out of you, reading about such behaviour.

. . . Oh, goodness, a final cautionary tale here from South Africa. It's a timely warning to all of you. Because, sadly, some victims don't seek my advice and instead plan their own revenge attacks.

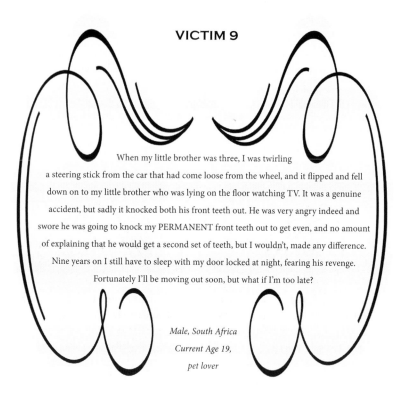

VICTIM 9

When my little brother was three, I was twirling a steering stick from the car that had come loose from the wheel, and it flipped and fell down on to my little brother who was lying on the floor watching TV. It was a genuine accident, but sadly it knocked both his front teeth out. He was very angry indeed and swore he was going to knock my PERMANENT front teeth out to get even, and no amount of explaining that he would get a second set of teeth, but I wouldn't, made any difference. Nine years on I still have to sleep with my door locked at night, fearing his revenge. Fortunately I'll be moving out soon, but what if I'm too late?

Male, South Africa
Current Age 19,
pet lover

Corinne: I'm going to accept this one was a genuine accident (don't make me regret trusting you, Mr X). I think, therefore, that I cannot pass sentence on you. The knowledge that you have lived the last nine years of your life in fear of surprise attacks from your little brother is sentence enough. Let's face it, you have probably lost pounds over the years, worrying about whether his birthday or Christmas presents contain an explosive device or if tonight will be the night that he flies out of your wardrobe at 4 a.m. No, I'm going to turn my attention to your little brother instead.

LET'S ALL FORGIVE

Now, little bro, I know you live some way from me, but I want you to picture us all holding hands. (Even then I'll mentally stand between you and your brother, just in case!) Once I have passed sentence I always recommend the singing of the Forgiveness Song. It's time to let this unfortunate event go. . . Join in and sing along with me now and feel the bitterness fly from your heart! Sadly, you can't actually hear me sing the melody, but I promise you it's haunting and, frankly, worthy of a record deal. So all of you victims above, and all the rest of you wronged individuals around the world, let's sing the words together:. . . . .

THE

FORGIVENESS

SONG

I WILL FORGIVE YOU — THOUGH YOU WERE MEAN
BUT LET'S NOT DWELL ON WHAT-HAS-BEEN.
LET US STAND TOGETHER — THOUGH YOU WERE UNKIND,
FOR A BETTER ....* YOU'D BE PUSHED TO FIND!

*\- please insert as
applicable: brother/
sister/family pet*

If you would like to hear how this song is sung and hear the illustrator, author, and even some of the characters in this book sing their forgiveness, this book is also available as an all-singing, all-dancing audiobook. Hope you like it!

You can find all the characters and Trucilla's own theme song on our special story CD/MP3 on amazon and itunes. And there is loads of colouring, and activities for schools and fun thingummybobs at www.trucilla.co.uk; you can tweet her at @trucillascake, or friend Trucilla Applegate on facebook, she insists you do!

Want even more laughs? From the same award-winning author and illustrator team, meet our much loved character 'RALPH'- the reluctant Superhero – and read all about his misadventures in the popular series: 'Ralph is (not) a Superhero' 'Ralph is (not) a Vampire' and 'Ralph is (not) a Spy'. Come and meet Ralph and his friends (and enemies!) at www.ralphisnotasuperhero.co.uk.

'Highly recommended junior school reading'
The School Library Association

THIS BOOK IS DEDICATED TO:

ALL AT THE UNIVERSITY OF THE ARTS, LONDON; TO MAGS AND OUR SUPPORT TEAM AT ROCKET-MIND, AND ESPECIALLY TO OUR EDITOR LYNN AND GRAPHIC DESIGNER KLARA FOR BRAVELY TACKLING ANOTHER CRAZY TALE! TO CORINNE'S LOVELY NIECES: SIÂN, MEGAN, EVIE AND LOTTIE, AND TO HER NEIGHBOURS FREYA AND MORVEN. . . NONE OF WHOM ARE ANYTHING LIKE TRUCILLA. ALSO TO EL'S GORGEOUS BRAND NEW NEPHEW VLADIMIR, HER (NOW WALKING) GODSON SEBASTIAN, NEPHEWS MAX AND OSCAR, TO THE PERFECT BABY, LEO, AND TO EL'S GORGEOUS (AND LONG-SUFFERING) SISTERS GEORGINA AND JANE. FINALLY TO ALL OF OUR FANS . . .

WE COULDN'T DO IT WITHOUT YOU!

CD & EA